To all those—people and dogs—
who go the extra mile to help others.
                                        —Debbie

To the University of Maryland Greenebaum Cancer Center, and
to Dozer, for changing the lives of so many. A special thanks goes to
Karen Warmkessel and Dr. Kevin Cullen for their help and support.
                                                        —Rosana

To Poppin, Django, and all of our furry friends out there.
                                        —David

Sleeping Bear Press gratefully acknowledges and thanks
Mr. Michael Greenebaum and Mr. Jon Sevel, co-founders of
the Maryland Half Marathon, and the University of Maryland
Greenebaum Cancer Center, Ms. Nona Nisman Greenebaum, and
Mr. Toby Hershkowitz for providing reference materials on
Dozer's half marathon run.

Text Copyright © 2014 Debbie Levy and Rosana Panza
Illustration Copyright © 2014 David Opie

Sleeping Bear Press®
315 E. Eisenhower Parkway, Suite 200
Ann Arbor, MI 48108
www.sleepingbearpress.com

Printed and bound in the United States.

10 9 8 7 6 5 4 3 2 1

Library of Congress Cataloging-in-Publication Data

Levy, Debbie.
Dozer's run : a true story of a dog and his race / written by Debbie Levy
and Rosana Panza ; illustrated by David Opie.
pages cm
Audience: Age 6-8.
ISBN 978-1-58536-896-9
1. Dogs—Maryland—Anecdotes. 2. Dogs—Maryland—Juvenile literature.
3. Human-animal relationships—Anecdotes. 4. Human-animal relationships—
Juvenile literature. I. Panza, Rosana. II. Opie, David, illustrator. III. Title.
SF426.5.L47 2014
636.7—dc 3   2013049581

Dozer's Run

A TRUE STORY OF A DOG AND HIS RACE

Written by Debbie Levy with Rosana Panza ✳ Illustrated by David Opie

It was a damp and drizzly Sunday morning in Dozer and Chica's neighborhood.

Who knew what delicious smells last night's rain washed in? Who knew what treasures the storm blew into the yard?

So the two best friends *str-e-tch-ed* out after a good night's sleep in the barn, shook themselves off, and began investigating.

The scent of squirrel here!

Out in the street, a runner ran by.

The fragrance of fox there! Traces of toad!

Then another runner.

And another and another and another and another…

Where were these runners running?

Dozer and Chica looked at each other.

Then they got back to their exploring.

Was this big branch here yesterday?

More runners ran by.

A raccoon was there!

Ahh, the whiff of wet wood ...

Frog, here in this hollow!

Where were all those runners running?

We stay in the yard, Chica said with her eyes.

Dozer's eyes were on the runners.

We belong in the yard, Chica's eyes said. *Plus, we haven't had breakfast yet. Later, we'll walk with our people.*

But the runners are running NOW, Chica, Dozer said with his big, swishy tail. *They must be chasing something wonderful!*

More wonderful than the flavor of frog and the reek of raccoon? More wonderful than breakfast, Dozer?

Dozer did love his breakfast.

But he had to find out what the runners were
chasing. He dashed out of the yard.

I'll be back, Chica!

Follow the leader!
But who was the leader?

Dozer followed his nose, and smelled…
a pocket full of gummies,
shorts with the scent of strange dog,
stinky socks,
tangy trail mix,
sneakers that once stepped in…never mind.

Dozer followed his ears. He heard...
Laughter! Whistles! *Wonderfulness!*

And lots of leaders.

Dozer could be a leader, too!

On and on the runners ran. On and on ran Dozer.

So much running was hard. A leader's job was to make it fun!
Dozer was good at fun.

How about a friendly game of chase? Dozer could outsprint everyone.

How about a game of tag?
No one could catch Dozer.

How about cooling off with a drink?
No one could slurp quite like Dozer.

Dozer had never run this much before. He grew tired and hungry.

Maybe there was breakfast at home!

Maybe he was done being a leader.

Dozer turned around. He started to run back.
He looked up into the faces of the other runners.

Everyone was happy to see Dozer.

Did a candy bar run by in that fanny pack?

The perfume of sweaty feet!

Jelly beans in that armband!

There was still so much to explore.

So Dozer turned around again.

Dozer kept his head high and his tail proud. Around him, people were drooping. Some were slowing down. These runners still needed him!

Come on!   One foot after another!   You can do it!

We'll be someplace wonderful soon!

Run, run, run, run, run!

Suddenly Dozer heard clapping and cheering.
He slowed down to investigate. He looked left.
He looked right. He looked straight ahead and …

OH!

Dozer sped up again and scampered across the finish line.

See?

I knew we could do it!
I knew we were running someplace wonderful!

The other runners smiled and chatted and high-fived. They all got big, shiny medals hung on broad ribbons. Their friends and family greeted them. Everyone was happy and proud.

But no one greeted Dozer. No one smiled and chatted and high-fived with Dozer. No one gave him a big, shiny medal.

No one even gave him a teeny, tiny dog treat.

Oh.

Suddenly this wasn't so wonderful.
It wasn't wonderful at all.

So—

Dozer ran on.

Morning turned into afternoon turned into evening.

There was no leader for Dozer to follow.
There were no followers for Dozer to lead.

Dozer was alone. He was alone all night long.

Monday was another damp and drizzly morning. Dozer's family had been searching for him and worrying ever since he sprinted out of the yard on Sunday. They came outside after a sleepless, sad night.

"Dozer! Dozer!"

"Come here, boy!"

"Come back, Dozer!"

"Here, Dozer!"

Dozer's mom looked and listened. But there was no sign or sound of Dozer.

There was only a dirty wet rag at the edge of the yard.

Then the dirty wet rag shook itself off and barked, ever so faintly.

DOZER!

Dozer's mom hugged him close.

Dozer limped to the barn. There was his bed. *That* was wonderful.

Dozer had his breakfast, at last. *Wonderfulness!*

Dozer plopped into his bed and fell asleep...

...for two days.

Thursday morning was *not*—finally!—another damp and drizzly one in Dozer and Chica's neighborhood.

The two best friends *stre-e-tch-ed* out. Then, as usual, they began investigating.

Opossum odor!

Tang of turtle!

The smell of slugs!

Aroma of—runner?

Aroma of *two* runners! These two men were in charge of the long race that Dozer had joined on Sunday. When they heard about the dog who had run practically the whole route, they just had to track Dozer down and pay him and his family a visit.

And they just had to give Dozer the prize that every runner who finished the thirteen-mile race earned: a big, shiny medal.

Also, some high-fives.

Dozer held his head up high and proud.

I did it, Chica! Dozer said with his tail. *I chased something wonderful, and I got it!*

Yes, Chica said with her eyes, *but I was worried.*

Oh.

Dozer put his head down a little. His nose caught the scent of something interesting on the ground.

This is wonderful, too, Dozer said with his tail.

And the two friends got back to exploring the wonderfulness of their own backyard.

Mmm! Bouquet of bunny rabbit here!

The skin of a snake there!

Vapor of vole!

Breakfast!

Author's Note

Dozer was three years old when he bolted from his yard in Highland, Maryland, to join the two thousand people running a race called the Maryland Half Marathon. He was definitely noticeable, trotting along nice and tall with his summer haircut and tail waving like a flag. Many runners assumed he was with one of the other human runners.

The two thousand people who participated in the thirteen-mile race that Sunday, May 15, 2011, had a special purpose. They ran to fight cancer. Each runner raised money to benefit the University of Maryland Greenebaum Cancer Center, which helps people with this disease.

Dozer hadn't run to fight cancer. A dog can't raise money!

Unless, that is, something wonderful happens.

After the race, word spread about Dozer. First one person made a donation to celebrate his run. Then another. And another and another and another. When all the donations were added up after the race on that cloudy spring morning, the total that Dozer raised was $25,000. This was twice as much as any other runner in the race. Dozer's donors—there were seven hundred of them—came from forty-three states, Canada, and Great Britain.

Dozer photo courtesy of Lydia Chandlee (a member of the Maryland Half Marathon committee)

Dozer went to the veterinarian right after his adventure. The vet pronounced him exhausted, but healthy. But running long distances without proper training is not a good idea for canines or humans. And a half marathon is really too strenuous for a Goldendoodle.

So after his big race, Dozer hung up his running shoes—or paws, to be exact. But although he gave up long-distance running, Dozer became the official Top Dog of the Maryland Half Marathon. He keeps raising money to fight cancer, as people keep donating money to celebrate him.

No one knows what Dozer did from the time he crossed the finish line before noon on Sunday until Monday morning, when he returned home. Did he stop and rest? Did he retrace his steps over the race route, running the half marathon in reverse? Or did he cut through fields and woods, parks and parking lots, backyards and front yards?

Similarly, no one knows exactly why Dozer found the Maryland Half Marathon so enticing. It was not in his nature to run away. He loved hanging out with his mom (okay, owner), Rosana Panza, her sons, Nick and Tyler, and Chica. Rosana says there was "a little miracle working within him" that day. Maybe Dozer won the hearts of so many people because he reminds us that anybody can create a "little miracle"—anybody can take steps, big and small, to help others.

You can see Dozer cross the finish line in a video online at: www.umgcc.org/news/marathon-dog.htm.